W9-BHH-273

Executive Producers: John Christianson and Ron Berry
Art Design: Gary Currant
Layout: Currant Design Group and Best Impression Graphics

Copyright © This Edition, 2002, Baby's First Book Club
Bristol, PA 19007
All rights reserved.
Text copyright © 1997, © 2002 Marcia Leonard
Art copyright © 1997, © 2002 Chris Sharp
Produced and published by Smart Kids Publishing, Inc.
ISBN 1-58048-293-7
Printed in China
No part of this book may be reproduced, copied, or utilized in any form or manner
without written persmission from the publisher. For information write to:
Smart Kids Publishing, Inc., 8403 Cliffridge Lane, La Jolla, CA 92037

Executive Producers: John Christianson and Ron Berry
Art Design: Gary Currant
Layout: Currant Design Group and Best Impression Graphics

HOW i FEEL

HAPPY

by Marcia Leonard
illustrated by Bartholomew

This little girl is painting a special picture.
She feels happy.

This little boy is happy, too.

He's the first one
to make tracks in the snow.

These kids are happy
just turning somersaults.

Have you ever felt that way?
Can you make a happy face?

This little boy is glad
because he found something
he thought was lost.

Do you have a favorite toy
that makes you happy?

These two kids are best friends.
They feel happy when they're together.

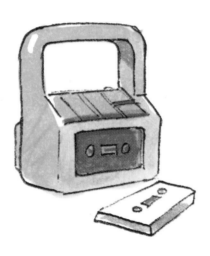

Is there someone you're always
glad to see?

This whole family is having
a wonderful time.

What does your family do
that makes you happy?

Sometimes happiness is
a warm, quiet feeling
that makes you smile.

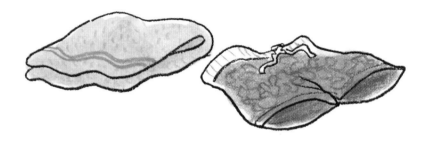

Sometimes it's a bubbly, tickly feeling
that makes you laugh.

You can make yourself happy
by doing things you like to do.

And you can make
other people happy, too.

Happiness is a feeling
you can share.

HOW I FEEL
Instructions

Use the How-I-Feel activity found in the back of this book to help your child explore the idea that emotions are change-able. Remove the chart and reusable stickers from the pocket. Ask your child to choose the face that matches how he or she is feeling—right now—and place it on the chart. Then ask your child to chose the face that shows how he or she would *like* to feel, and place that sticker on the chart, too. Are the faces the same or are they different? Use the How-I-Feel chart several days in a row and talk about how feelings can change.